DRIVING THE CELEXA
By Miriam Stanley

- A Single Volume.
- 120 pages.
- Trade Paperback.
- American contemporary poetry collection by a single author.

Rogue Scholars Press
http://www.roguescholars.com

Design and Layout: C. D. Johnson
Publishers: Rogue Scholars Press

ISBN-10: 0-9840982-7-5
ISBN-13: 978-0-9840982-7-9

Published by Rogue Scholars Press
New York, NY - USA

DRIVING the CELEXA

Miriam Stanley

Published by Rogue Scholars Press
www.roguescholars.com

This book is dedicated to my father, Jonathan Israel Rosenfeld, Bernie Sanders, Iris N. Schwartz, and to C. D. Johnson.

This is also dedicated to my late cat, NV.

CONTENTS

CONTENTS Continued

APPENDIX

What can I say, my dear reader, that can inform or motivate you? I guess I can repeat what Siddhartha Buddha said, WITH OUR THOUGHTS WE MAKE OUR WORLD.

With that wisdom, here are five of my most frequent thoughts:

1. Get enough batteries for the climate apocalypse. Remember to stockpile matzah in Tupperware. Matzah has a long shelf life.

2. Watching the evening news is like stopping to watch a five - car pile-up.

3. Olivia Benson from Law and Order is a middle-aged, smart, tough, female superhero. Of course, she will retire. Then there will nothing to watch on TV.

4. Being Jewish is exhausting. Fortunately, my cats don't judge me for my faith.

5. Napping is a good hobby.

My world tells you to prepare for emergencies, respect female superheroes, and adopt a cat. That's pretty good advice.

Enjoy the poems.

———

Dad was first published in the **Riverside Poets Anthology** (Volume 15) by Flabbergasted Press.

Something Larger Than Oneself was first published in the **Riverside Poets Anthology** (Volume 16) by Flabbergasted Press, 2016.

Electric Bed was first published in the **Riverside Poets Anthology** (Volume 16) by Flabbergasted Press, 2016.

Harmonica was first published in the **Riverside Poets Anthology** (Volume 16) by Flabbergasted Press, 2016.

Arthritis was first published in **Palabras Luminosas**, by Rogue Scholars Press, 2016.

Aftermath

He got a call. Took a train.
A young servant waited at the platform.
The man led him across the *platz*.
Pointed out the infamous building.
Alone, Joe climbed the stairs.
The old woman at the top knew no English;
She pantomimed tragedy:
His 'ex' had opened the fifth floor chute that
Leads to the furnace.
Crawled in, got stuck, a hairball in a sink pipe.
Her wide, sexy hips propped between those narrow walls
Unable to birth her.

Now, her brain mangled,
She couldn't recognize her own dog.

Joe visited with flowers;
The hospital chaplain standing close by.
Judging him like Jesus. Judging her, too.
Life grows its gnarled branches and Man has the hack-saw.

Eventually, Joe leaves.
Boards the noon train under the cover of downpour.
The prerequisite visit throbbing in his ribcage.
Like his former lover once stuck, unable to be dislodged
Inside her agony.

———

The Age I Am

I grew up clueless.
Before HIV had its label.
A hidden seed growing, not yet discovered.
First, a fellow student got pneumonia. Left St. Vincent's wards, still clutching
A tissue.
Three years later the college made a scholarship in his name.
When the diagnosis appeared, it mobilized our neighborhood of artists.
It stood more dangerous, more powerful that the mayor.
We went to rehab,
Moved upstate,
Hunkered down,
Some of us fled to Jersey.
The virus followed like packed, giant luggage.
Like a river overflowing its banks.

———————

Miriam Stanley

AIDS Poem

Thank God, I didn't go to that party.
Thank God, I didn't meet George.
Thank God, I never knew how cute he was, and how witty
George was that night.
Thank God, I didn't sleep with him.
Thank God, I was working full-time and married.
Thank God, my husband never cheated.
But God hid His face when sweet, funny George gasped for breath.
When he was on the Hickman catheter.
When the gentle nurse who took care of him
Slept with the wrong person, and then she died.
And when a teacher passed away in the next ward.
Yes, God Hid his face.
He hid His face from Jews praying in the death camps.
He hid His face from nuns raped in El Salvador.
Hid His face on black worshipers shot from the gunfire of congealed hate.
Gd hid His face from the swollen stomach attached to twiglike limbs, who was
the body of a starving baby.
He has replied "no" to the most generous.
The most faithful.
The most considerate.
Yet I thank Gd.
I was very, *very lucky*.

_____

Alchemy

Peroxide burning in. Its acrid scent on plastic gloved hands; the bathroom
Silent as an egg.

Drips of dye staining floor grout;
Inky drops flung on toilet bowl, old towels,
The corners of my forehead darkened red.
Forty minutes steeping grey in sepia glop.

Then other goop, albumen white, to fix color.
'Set it' like a photograph.

Then the rinsing. Fingers caressing scalp with shampoo;
Strands falling out; watery chemicals
Feeding the drain.

Then, hugging him. Joy wrinkles my eyes.
Crow's feet tighter than rivets. I kiss his
Bald head.

———————

All Footage: A Grainy Black And White

The bursting cloud of smoke:
A dissipating confusion.
We, the viewers, see details emerge.
The rubble settles.
A woman in a hijab, perhaps a nurse,
Now crumpled fabric in a corner.
The patients, the beds: covered in debris.
The last maternity hospital in Aleppo gone in shambles.

Like faces collapse in sobs,
On people crowded on the SS St. Louis,
Spooled back across the Atlantic.
Sent to their deaths; Nazi Germany
Swallowing up rejected Jewish refugees.
Families in the maw of the monster.

These crossroads of filmed horror re-enacted
Through season and memory. We watch the doomed while
We eat dinner; the thermostat at seventy degrees.

———————

Always

There are scratches on the walls of the gas chamber.
Claw marks made by the gasping, trying to dig their way out.
Almost a graffiti obscene to visitors.
The hands, the nails, digging into condemned throats dry and hot as ovens.

And today, once again, children gasp for air.

They are on the floor, fish flopping on the beach of battle, wide-eyed, brown
irises with dilated pupils.

They claw the air, grasp for dead mothers, or angels, or the doctors that crouch
Over them with oxygen masks.

The children, this time, are Syrian, Arab, Muslim; does it matter?

My relatives clench the hems of my mind, their corpses alive in my dreams.
These relatives also gassed. Grey...stiff...naked.

I go on the internet. Email my senators. Type in uppercase: WE HAVE TO DO
SOMETHING.

I never hear back. Words fall into a dark space filled with bodies.

———————

Aryan Nation

It was Englewood versus Westwood.
One team mostly black, the other team white.
I cheered for the Englewood team, pissing off
Westwood's blondes.
They reminded me of the Farrah Fawcett wannabes
That stole my confidence and never gave it back.
Englewood was the long shot with less wins this season.
I loved them more than pizza.
In the third quarter, Westwood made a touchdown –
The first for either team.
Westwood cheerleaders wiggled their asses.
Their texting parents duly applauded.
In the last quarter, Westwood made two more goals;
Englewood chased the ball the feckless way I used to run laps.
The Englewood fans simply packed up.
From two blocks off, I heard the Englewood band play.
The drums receded in sound slowly: a dying heartbeat.

———————

Bagging And Sagging

It's no done much, anymore.
But there's still some kids that do it.
Their belts unusable. The jean's waist at their hips. The underwear showing, or worse,
The crack of their buttocks. One elder quips to them, "Pull up your pants; crack kills!"

I tell them, "It looks like you took a dump."

Never mind. These kids don't listen. Hopefully, they'll change when they apply
For a job. Appear before a disapproving employer who crosses his arms and grunts, "Come back when you're dressed for work."

Kids... Many 'not-so-bad.' Just unaware, clueless as yesteryear's hippies.

Walking these streets, sometimes posturing a 'gansta roll'; holding groceries for beloved Grandmas while holding up the top of their oversized jeans.

That awkward performance.

Bingo

My sister won fifty dollars and the old men said how great Dad was.
Mom won nothing.
But she beamed, hearing our father praised.
This was the third day of *shiva**, only she was playing Bingo instead.
Cancer, the world's worst burglar, robbed her of eight months of joy.
But Dad's now safe; he's resting in peace. Mom doesn't have to worry about his
Suffering.
The Rabbi said Dad is in Heaven: as Mom's concerned, she can play Mahjong as
Well.
The future is open as a window.
When she rubbed her husband's feet his last day of life, her fate was earned:
The shape of things to come.

———————

*Shiva is the Jewish period of mourning.

Borderline Personality Disorder

She carved the word *ugly* on her left arm,
Then vomited until spitting blood.
Bright red splashes in the sink under the light.
She glides in grey territory
Where symptoms come and go:
Fellow travelers on a bridge
Where danger has no markers and
Perpetrators are kings.

The nurses tell her to hold ice cubes instead
When she wants to cut.
To let the cold seep through her palms,
Into fingers, the searing pain blocking out all emotions,
Like a transformer or a switch.

After that, she runs in place for five minutes.
Building exhaustion; elbows flying up and down,
A wind-up doll panting, chest heaving, the mouth gulping air.

Feelings now distant; she outran them.
The past is back behind.
Memory far, far away from the present.
The body is now safe.
She hums if the voices come back.
The methods are endless...

———————

Brazen For Bernie, 2016

She pressed the buzzers.
I stared at the name list.
When someone walked out on the ground floor,
We smiled and let ourselves in.
Two Jewish girls. Two skinny, 'nice-Jewish- girls'.
Greeting "Good morning"
Lathered in daytime cheer.
Nodding to the tenants who naively
Held open the door.
We invaded the buildings,
Intruding on apartments clustered like
Trees on top of hills.
We went from floor to floor,
Shoving oak tag Bernies over doorknobs,
Like a hundred do-not-disturb signs. Spoke to tenants
About where to vote.
Schmoozed politics
Ten a.m. Saturday to millennials
Holding laundry.
After we had snuck into every building
It was time to go home.
We had triumphed with our fair complexion.
Used our 'privilege' for good.

_____

Brenda

I need to wrestle the past until it cries uncle.
But it is like grappling water, the memory hazy.
Mom's face a shifting pail of quicksand;
She insists I "enjoy" the mall.
My father drives me there like I'm Miss Daisy.
I clutch him, picture the crowd circling, forming a net.
I moan; he drives me back...
Then I take my pills and sit in a chair.
I am a popped balloon.
Watching a sitcom, then another.
My parents argue inside the kitchen.
They are distant as Lee attacking Grant.
Remote as Greece attacking Troy.
Later, Dad drives me to the clinic; I am silent in the back.
Innocent cargo.

_____

Bucket List

Some people have the Grand Canyon.
Others pick visiting Disney.
I have silver Doc Martin boots,
With David Bowie charm.
Some stardust from Mars flaked over its skin.
Silver ink printed on leather, fragile as rice paper.
A large tag warns Do Not Rub,
Don't even polish.
I wear them with anxiety when on the crowded subway.
They are for my niece's wedding. Planned for Newport.
The Trump supporters crowding around, martinis in hands,
Lobster Bisque in porcelain on glass tables.
My niece in virgin lace. The train held by a Yale graduate.
I am thrift shop chic, strutting old aunt craziness across the sandy lawn.
My boots glittering under the sun.
The heels, the treads, solid as Bernie Sanders.
My brain soaked in vodka's formaldehyde.

———————

The Cancer Poems: Part One

We'd talk about constipation.
Over and over.
Like when he pooped. How much? How can we help him poop?
Later, we'd discuss Colace and bran.
When we were not in the room, he was ensconced on the toilet, but sat helpless as a latke.
There's an old Yiddish curse: *Gai kaken oifen yam*:
"Go crap in the ocean."
We'd ask, "Did you to the ocean today,"
"Should we drive you to the beach?"
"We're going to Point Pleasant; who wants to visit?"
Punchlines spread like wine stains. Dad said we can charge money.
Dad...
Pale, his voice a falsetto pulled through the reed of fatigue. Hooked up to shunts, oxygen tanks, clear tubes, and a nebulizer mask that he joked "smelled like cappuccino."
My mother starving and quiet;
Her appetite suspended until he comes home.

————————

Chana's Conscience
(Inspired from events of Chanukah)

This I know:
I did my job.
I calmed the boys that shook.
I gathered the seven in a big bouquet.
"Here G-d," I said,
"Take them."
I watched them like whales pushed back to sea.
Heaven waited in the other room.

———————

Channeling My Inner Joey Ramone

My hair lies limp as a dead animal.
Draped over my head.
The carcass hanging flat to its edges.
Dark and somber as a Soviet soul.
I'm walking around with it,
Advertising my disinterest in beauty salons.
"You must love me," I say to the world,
"For my personality."
At Spring, the strands frizz, recreating
The Black Forest,
The static garlanding the scalp with chaos.
Yet still, I avoid hair products.
Childhood years of solitude and an adolescence
With acne, made me embrace my inner
Patti Smith and Joey Ramone,
Glowing deep inside like Plutonium.

———————

The Conference

He said she bled like a shot horse.
But he had sex with her anyway.
The maid would clean the room.
Carry the soiled linen and pillows discretely down to
The basement like sheets from an OR.
And despite her penchant for baby talk,
And ripe, vermillion sap coating his member,
He shook, then buckled faster than a tasered mule.

Later they put back on their name tags, dangling from
Key chains.
Schmoozed corporate gossip while slipping into their shoes.
Him, gingerly polite, laughing at her jokes,
Skillfully bandaging her exposed, feminine ego.
Complimenting her post-committee seminar.
She, of course, knowing he won't call.
With cautiously gentle repartee,
they walk to the elevator.

————————

The Corporate Cafeteria

Dedicated to Aunt Rifka

"I couldn't try Rich; he would break me in half;
Look at his hands. Look at his shoes!"

"Now, Michael is really creative;
I bet he would try anything."

"How about Lonely Larry? You want a man who's grateful."

Silence folds on the chatter.
The women resume eating.
Playing with dressing-soaked salad on
Styrofoam plates in that desultory
Method of dieters.
Ladies of 'a certain age' having worked an endless flood of years;
Sporting dyed hairdos and overstuffed pocketbooks.
Plodding for 401K's like trained seals waiting for fish.

"Well, I guess we should finish our lunch,"
Sighs the 'winter-wheat' blonde.
"Lonely Larry called a staff meeting."

_____

Dad

He's clawing the oxygen mask and
The Biovac that keeps him breathing.
A tube snakes out of this penis with urine
Grey-yellow seeping through plastic
Running into the bag. It's all ugly and Mom
Runs to get a nurse.

After the shot of Ativan, the delirium stops; he's
A corpse still alive; monitors crowding the bed. The
Diastolic hovers on fifty. "That's pretty good,"
The doctor says – one of many doctors – as well as
Respiratory therapist, housekeeping aide,
And nutritionist – that walk in and out.

Of course, the food tray stays untouched; Dad stopped
Swallowing a day ago. Around the time he last talked.
We asked, "soup?" He gasped "yes." We raised the cup
To his lips but liquid dribbled, and the watermelon
Bite stuffed his jowls, until parts went down
His throat and he coughed: the nurse said it went down
The wrong pipe. After this, he stopped eating.

This is just as well; the oxygen mask was almost
Always on and his mouth gaped open like a
Drowned man: His belly distended, welled against
The blanket.

I knew it was late: any day now, but Mom
Said, "Don't call anyone; don't ruin their weekend."
When he finally slipped into a coma, when his heart
Finally stopped, Mom cried once again into my sister's arms.
Clutched the daughter who was her sustenance.

After that, the two rode back to the retirement village.
I sat *shiva** in New York. And the movie played on
With plenty of extras: his poker buddies, the bocce club, the
Rabbi in Teaneck.
With the one person who held my family together, now gone.

_____

**Shiva* is the Jewish custom of mourning

DC- 37

In the clinic, social work hears
Benefits are cut,
Our pensions threatened,
That the cafeteria is privatized
That food for patients is ordered by an outside vendor....
That DC-37 sat on its ass when Wendy workers went out on strike.
Now I see old age as cold weather: no gas,
Tatting the vestiges of social security into a budget.
Union dues vanish like released balloons into the clouds.

Sometimes I see the world through nightmares:
People in shacks bottling Coca-Cola,
Women in saris sweating in crammed rooms.
I see DC-37 chopped into pieces-
Collective bargaining the first to go...

I recall my father soaring with the sun, 1969,
Striking with the teachers; Al Shankar kicking tail In the background.

I know Barclay Street staff buys lunch at Whole Foods;
Sips cappuccino,
Orders 2000 more T-shirts
To parade at City Hall: painter's caps as an added note...
I lose calcium, cartilage, mobility:
I am losing even my teeth.
I buy a bridge to span gaps in an inflamed mouth.
I pay out of pocket.

———————

Deluge

I

A flood of voices rain down. They are the thoughts in her head.
She wields the blade against her throat before her brother enters the room.
His nails dig crescents into her fists: she clutches the handle; it is a rope
Lifting her out of the world.
She opens her mouth. Screams, "I'm not Mrs. Phillips." The mother calls EMS.
The girl writhes in the arms of childhood, rejecting the heartbreak of a bad marriage.
As if memory can be stripped like old clothes. Yellow voices railing their demands,
Her breath: labored as overworked mules, the heart racing to an unknown, distant finish line.
Her brother smokes weed in the next room; he's tired of saving her.

II

It is quieter now, the voices lulled to her own stupor.
The emergency room: far back. Its doors a maw of suffering letting in more
Suffering.
A family coagulated around a loved one screened by police.
She is elsewhere: in the extended occupancy beds. Colors a picture in the
Activity Room,
The Plexiglas: a giant mother. It swaddles her while she is blanketed in meds...
The beauty of the ebbing sound...like a hotel blocks from the coast; the bare
closet, the door without Keys...
Just a murmur.

III

1963: She's born.
1993: Hope lifts with the dress. The hem skirting over innocent eyes that turn
into something else...The man who does this...She is in Jamaica – an aphid in
her family garden.
Then she's gone.
2007: Walking down streets in Miami. Sundry locations. Anonymous, barefoot.
A female officer approaching...

31

IV

The next chapter in her torn story:
I am Mrs. Phillips, born Miss Padmore. I used to style hair at a solon called Miss
Mary's at St. Elizabeth Parish. By the port once known for shipwrecks. I studied
to sixth form, my
Clothes ironed and white. Now I live in East New York, traveling by way of
Florida.
Just call me the name I was christened – Rachel.

_____

Denise

The stretched knit pulls against rolls of belly fat.
She taps painted nails on her thigh, then his.
He fiddles with his belt; she's naked before his shoes drop.
Later, she punches a shopkeeper; the EMS blares, the cops arrive. They drive
Her to emergency room. City workers type on the computer; she's some
Doctor's problem now.
Nurses offer meds, smog-blue pajamas; she bends into a cot, smashes a
Blotchy, left cheek into the anorexic pillow.
She still has acne.
I sigh at my new charge. We met twice before.
I ask, "What clinic do you attend?" She winces, twists the sheet into a veil over
Her eyes, spiraling into the black hole of dopamine and benzos, neurons
Flushing like a toilet.
I wait over her: a suitor completely rejected and keeping her from a nap.
Silently, I curse K2.

_____

The Drill

I wanted to join a commune
And folk dance.
I was six.
Coloring the letter B.
When the siren rang
We all moved from our desks,
Lined up in the hall,
Hands clasped behind our ponytails,
Eyes facing the cinder block walls of
Robertsville Elementary.
Didn't know Russian warheads;
Just wet, green jungle,
In a place called Vietnam by Walter Cronkite.
I knew China made delicious lo mein and something
Called Pu-Pu platter right off route 9 at the China Buffet.
When we ambled back to our seats,
Mrs. Montalto leaned her aching spine
Against the blackboard;
White chalk silently ruining her silk mini.
Dust smeared on that spectacular yellow.
What a disaster.

———

Electric Bed

Magic.
Gifted.
The room incandescent.
You switched on every lamp:
Con Edison your slave.
The bathroom light is on. Towels used, wet, on the floor,
Terry cloth servants all exhausted...
After five minutes the bed is still. You dig in your bag.
The shades are down as Miles Davis.
You put another quarter in the slot,
And current screams all over the frame;
The bed again, "on," shivering like a swimmer,
Rocking your prone body with industrial DTS; you vibrate in the
Econolodge Shangri-La as its CEO, viceroy, general,
A low-maintenance doge; you are the Jersey Boy dauphin,
Shaken like a Waldoff martini; you thank Shakti, Devi, and Shiva,
Your limbs all in the tune with Tesla,
Once again happy to be alive
For at least fifteen minutes.

———————

The Fifth Avenue Synagogue Burns

Stockbrokers cry into delicate palms.
Doctors weep in front of doormen.
The orange rain slings wood and masonry;
A thicket of hoses weaves through fire trucks
And soon the chaos is gone.

Politicians arrive for their *shiva* call;
The camera crews circle;
There are two million Jews in New York.

Mom hopes it's arson - a hate crime.
For us Jews to be victims again.
To eclipse Bernie Madoff
And the West Bank settlers.
-     Those eternal embarrassments
that burn like arthritis.

She wants a white supremacist,
-     Please Gd, let him be a cop -
Mailing a ninety page manifesto. Festooned in red ink.
Swamped in swastikas. His fervent love letter to Fox News.

———————

For The Duration

He was her first man. Only man.
She was sitting by his bed. Perched in a wide chair made smaller by her
Crumpled coat. She had been in the room three days without a shower.
Mom was The Sentry. Observer. Courtier. The Messenger with the wrinkled
Shirt, who never leaves.
We tried to coax her out of the room but she wouldn't budge.
Dad was ensconced in the hospital bed; the mattress cranked up; his back
Encased in pillows like a raj in India staring at his immense fields.
Mom: "No, I don't want to eat."
So I call the social worker. A plump woman comes to talk to my mother; first
She mentions she's going to Israel.
Mom excitedly recommends hotels, but "No", she won't have lunch.
Finally, I go downstairs to get her a yogurt.
Dad is nodding off. His oxygen was at eighty percent, so his doctors increased
The pressure of the nozzle. He has blood clots in his lungs.
And I see Mom in a race to get sick as Dad.
She *can't* survive him.

———————

Friend's Birthday Party

The bread tastes of oil and garlic.
The hard crust, the thick center.
The olive scent that conjures twisted branches and gnarled trees.
Oh the groves, how distant with their tanned farmers!
But now I'm chewing the bread like chewing cud.
The tough slices bedded in a spectacular basket,
Nested on thick paper.
I am savoring all this as well as the strong, dark coffee.
There is nothing else to eat; everything is *treyf*.*
And I'm at a Sicilian restaurant with my best friend named Tenerelli.
Forbidden wine and meat, and stringy, hot cheese scattered like diamonds.
Along with the basil marinara.
Oh G-d, reward me; remember this day! Put it in Your front pocket in Your
'To-do' list. Remember the sights, the aromas, the clatter of used, now-empty
Plates. Recall these hours like an old, outstanding bet waiting to be cashed in.
Remember me as a waiter brings *everyone else* dessert: Oh, the tiramisu, the
Birthday cake!
—

*Treyf means 'not kosher'.

___

40

Getting Attention From The Russians

You need to send a selfie.
Wear something lacy, showing dollops of flesh.
I heard this worked for Jeff Sessions.
Don't send your poems;
They are scraps Putin will throw away.
Like sleeping with your professors,
Or your last boss,
You have to *work* this.
Buying the right costume to go to the ball.
Surfing intrigue with your gullet engorged with beluga.
Don't you know their secrets are better than diamonds?
Your soul melts from an elixir brewed from Crimean potatoes.
Till your face is in symbiosis with the oak floor.
You thought you were Mata Hari.
You're worse than a Vladivostak whore.
A dog learning new tricks from a sweaty, overweight
Apparatchik.

_____

Gilded Age

Peeling tectonic plates off the face of the earth.
But no, *linoleum* off pressed fiberboard.
Back aching from what my doctor warned me to avoid.
Crouching like a dinosaur in a swamp: lumber discs arched over vinyl.
Hammer banging soundwaves through a neighbor's wall.
I'm Frank Gehry,
Richard Hunt,
Stanford White.
A long-time tenant saving a rent-stabilized mess.
On Twenty-fifth and Second.
As the rich kids storm in.
From Northport and Deal.
Having smug parents that ignore me.

I sit on my doughy buttocks.
Dream up a world gleaned from photos of *The Gilded Age*.
I own nothing but my mind.
And *who admires that*?

I remember a man who breathed sonnets,
Murmured in four languages,
Who said I'm heroic, strong, and
Precious as silk.
Years before he moved,
And I am popping more Advil,
Patching my life,
Poem after poem,
Tile after tile,
Square after square.

———

Grocery

The one place I can grab anything I want.
The aisles near like suitors while
I approach them.
This perfect dance,
This magical dance,
Where I am never rejected.

I reject them:
The laundry soap with phosphorus.
The costly, imported vinegar.
The chocolate-covered pecans that become slivers between teeth.

Then, I glide to the next aisle, as
The Queen of Tomato Sauce, The
Princess of Rice, Her Royal Highness of Pickled Artichokes.
Ah, this is power!

Able to return to that 'palace' of a studio basement,
Free from the boss, clear of timesheets,
Gulping macaroni over the TV tray,
While watching re-runs of *Law and Order*.

Dagastinos: The BFF of the twenty-first century.

———

Happy Family Take-Out

It used to be on Third Avenue.
Between 24th and 25th.
The other side, flanked by a bodega.
The cooks of Happy Family in plain sight, sliding the chow Mein in a wok, the
Pop of broth mixing with grease. The soot behind the alley, adjacent to the old
Foundry.
That spot gone, along with the bodega, but now there's chilled Chablis sold in a
Wine café, sanded floors gleaming, Danish blonde, freshly waxed.
The new tenants of the neighborhood sip, girls perfectly toned, hair waved
like Greek sails. Teeth clomp down on each biting comment. As Piranhas. Bear
traps. Words caught like krill in a whale. Over white, linen tablecloths made in
Egypt.
Low-lit rooms wafting coriander.
"I fired the magazine's photography department; brought in my own people."
The soft sound of fresh success.

———————

Harmonica

I have a plastic harmonica still untouched in plastic wrap.
Spare change surrounds it.
Everything in a drawer, in a kitchen, joined by dust bunnies and closets.
This mouth organ I never played. Stuck in a hand before getting arrested.
For marching around an empty plaza in circles.
In front of a closed courthouse on a Saturday.
Superfluous loops, uneventful until the riot police showed up.
Batons, helmets, orange plastic netting, megaphone.
I was cuffed and brought to the paddy wagon,
With the officer lugging my handbag.
No melodies summoned, no instruments. Though in the van, some prisoners' wrists wiggled free.
A great-grandmother found a cell phone. Six mouths waited while taking turns, reaching a loved one through pilfered contraband.
Focused in fear, leaving a message.
No one humming a tune in protest.

_____

Hot Coffee

Death is a long sword covered with everyone's blood.
Ubiquitous as a Seattle umbrella.

Yet hot coffee warms the throat and hand,
My body under the silk blanket.
And there's the feathery pages of an old paperback.
The gentle fiction; the soft weight.

In June, I lost my father so
Now I read Gogol.

The Overcoat, The Buyer of Souls, all the Ukrainian references
Piling up like baklava.
Villages, taverns, provincial clerks – lit under the crystal lamp on my
Pine nightstand.

Dad suffered for eight months
Riddled with tumor.
Later, his flesh donated to science.

I squint through green blinds, in the midst of typing a poem.
The room breathes with sleeping cats.
It is the weekend; there is no work.
It is bright September in a quiet city.
A candle wafts lavender.

———————

I Say

Life is better when you are grown.
Joan shrugs, "How?"
I say you'll have a locked door. Own room,
Own kitchen,
Can soak like a turnip in a private tub.
Order delivery from a local deli; eat pastrami with dripping hands.
Eat salad without a fork.
"Sure," She sighs. The teen slouches deeper into the chair.

I don't add that life is more often a commuter train.
Without an empty seat in July. Armpits and bad breath everywhere.
Stench rising like flooded sewage, occupying your rumbling confinement,
Disgust flowers like Satan's bouquet, then a stranger approaches
preaching you're going to Hell. Quotes loudly from
Revelations. Stares down at your cleavage.
No-frills, low-budget, hypocritical loathing.

Life: a ceaseless shuttle of senseless suffering, with moments of rest.

_____

Miriam Stanley

It Was A Week After The Election

With accusations in the office.
Someone "voted for that fascist";
Someone else "voted communist".
And as the weeks crept to the feared inauguration,
Friends congealed into crowds:
Streams of placards and megaphones on puddled streets.
Fists rising over the slush.
Women's rights, immigrants' rights, the rights of various races, and
The adolescent imperative of making the inevitable stop.
I was at home, lugging the indifference
Of a full belly and just-cracked book.
A cold draft seeping through two windows
And a plate glass door.
And you swathed in three layers of wool,
Spoke of relatives long dead, killed eighty years ago,
Mentioned there is nothing horrific a politician hasn't done yet.
Genocide a single frame of a film set on your face.
We talked of Aleppo.

———————

Jack In The Box

You have to crank the handle a few rotations
Before I pop up.
Otherwise, the firm, tin walls are a shelter,
Enamel stripes painted on their surface.
A box eight by eight by eight inches,
I sit safe inside.
Peaceful, before you mess with the hidden gears.
Then you scream, giggle when I jump from the open lid.
Me, helpless, tethered to a pin, a shackled prisoner
In front of your overwhelming size.
An object in your soft, stubby hands.
Your fingers that just handled a wedge of cake
Or the silky skin of your mother.

———

Karl Marx Speaks...

They say I had a blind spot the size of Prussia.
Looming larger than my Jewish past.
That I strode over Man's Greed like a puddle
I expect to evaporate.
Couldn't see each serf wants to run his own manor.
That most poor don't aspire to share,
Whether fate, land, or fortune.
But how would I know sipping Riesling in Berlin?
Ah yes, a human being is really a sinkhole.
Swallowing items.
Acquiring refuse.
Grinding up mountains up in his voluptuous maw.
Humanity: a feral metropolis of cats seeking their corners.
I thought the proletariat would mimic the factory.
All parts working in tandem, labors aligned as gears;
The masses a well-oiled machine.
How was I to know about the ambition of the shop clerk?
Each peasant more unpredictable than weather?
Each scullery maid's soul building a border wall.
The miller, the blacksmith, the cobbler dreaming a
Palace in their heads.
I was a bird looking down from the rarified air,
Soaring with my aristocrat wife;
Each beggar the size of an ant.

———

Leaving A Man

When you leave a man, you abandon districts.
Soon he rebuilds, and now you are a *fallen kingdom*.
He anoints statues to a new woman.
Your artifacts reserved for the catacombs.
You are the scattered femurs below the rocks,
Under the bridge,
Possessing no angels.
You are the broken promise.

————

Life On Walton's Mountain

The day John Boy married, I cried in the living room. I leaned against the
Painted, plaster cupids. Their gold lampshades. Their nylon tassels.
Dreamt of a four poster bed. The lucky girl's blood stain.

Mom yelled at me to get downstairs. She had lamb chops. They taste
"VERY" bad when they're cold. They're "VERY" expensive. I ran down after
Drying my eyes. Everyone asked why they're red.

I loved John Boy's horse eyes, and the way he could build a shelf. His
Mouth tightly shut when he hammers. A determination rare as tintype.
The way he lugged logs down Walton's mountain. How he damn near *never*
Complained.

When I moved from New Jersey, I was in love with Spock. I wanted to live
On the Starship Enterprise. Share his cabin. Touch his buff body. Travel in tow
With this genius through galaxies. He had a Vulcan grip, training, and
experience.
He was smarter than Alex Trebek. He was a good listener. Perfect for a long
marriage.

———————

Maggid

The Passover ritual where Jews tell of getting freedom from slavery in Egypt).
We Jews drip wine out of Seder cups.
When listing the Ten Plagues.
Curbing joy about our enemies' death.
Leashing the smugness of victory
So, too, I clam-up when hearing my boss was laid-off.
The Sphinx with the 'American Gothic' mouth.
The Darth Vader of staff evaluations.
Appraising us underlings incompetent.
Security escorted her back to her desk.
Her shrunken, shaking figure given
Ten minutes to gather four years of accrued contents.
Her password gone; her email blocked.
Pharaoh forced us Jews to make bricks.
Without straw.
Some ancient, fucked up mind game.
Some oppressors really ask for it.
Word came down that she was accompanied into the parking lot.
Guarded like classified garbage.
Her office door sealed, too.
The scene of her manifold crimes.
Oh Master of the Universe, forgive me for gloating!

———————

Mall

A consolation prize for the lonely.
The isolated. The bored.

Wandering like deer in a forest.
Foraging on aisles.
Killing time off the food court.
Next to the pseudo-waterfall,
Pumped off of fake rocks.

While you with your mom,
Search for green bridal wear,
For the wedding of a cousin you despise.

Buying a beaded monstrosity you will return in three days.
Burning a college kid on commission
When cooing to her the fib, "I decided not to attend".
Smearing your grin all over her face.
Making it even harder for her to pay tuition.
This is all just Chinese boxes of phony,
Russian nesting dolls of pain.
Complete with parking lot.
The sadness sits in the air, brewing.

Benches encircle with backless seats.
Now

———

The Martian Chronicles

When I read about the crystal cities,
emerald spires,
sand canals,
the gold, bronze eyes hammered flat as
veal cutlets

When I dream of the blue ships sailing
through the cool, Martian seas.

When I feel the breeze,
hear the tinkle of bells,
the telepathy keeping the mouth shut.

Brooklyn is 300 pages away.

I close the musty paperback.

Conjuring the Dewey Decimal System on
inked, oak tag. Labels slipped into the
three by five, nickel frames.
Treasures: 800 for poetry, 900 for nonfiction,
titled alphabetized in a narrow drawer's card catalog.
Held in tunnels of nailed wood
in a pigeon-drawered, walnut cabinet.

Memories of magical searches - found joy – when I was small,[
powerful with future.

_____

My Father's Marks

An inked X on each foot. Nurses say, "To mark the pulse of his extremities."
Both ankles swollen, raging red: Dad's body fighting for its life.
Mom sobs, "Your father is only seventy-eight." I say nothing.
She fiddles with the cell phone, still doesn't know how to use it. I look at her
neglected hair, her eyes looking for a nurse to say, "This is just a setback".
That quiet sanctuary of fiction that she and my sisters always crawl into, leaving
the doomed man to suffer radiation, surgery, and chemo while I circle the
rooms, my eyes gazing out the window.
The stigmata of memory.

———————

My Moroccan Boyfriend

Eats bacon in front of my face.
Although I am Jewish.
Even though he is Muslim.
I guess he thinks taboos are broken
so *let's shatter them all*.
But I cluck loudly,
worse than his mother.
I rebuke, "Don't you keep anything?"
He smiles, looks back at his skinny, cute
hypocrite.
"I first ate bacon when I was at Rutgers.
It's so good, so cheap."
The man resumes chewing.
I resume looking at his bovine neck.
The way he leans forward to take his knife.
A glutton in everything, and for this I am lucky.

———————

Promised Land

Next week, you fly to Lebanon
To a refugee camp
Of a thousand Palestinians.
To drive two dozen children
With a dozen binoculars, to see
beyond a patrolled border.
Frustrated as Moses
On Mount Nebo,
Gazing upon Canaan.
Legs twitching with desire to
Run in, weave through cyclomens.
Later you teach the teens English
Guiding them from the Gordian knot of politics,
To pass entrance exams.
You are barely twenty two,
And three thousand years old.

———

Queen N.E.R.D.

Better than ex-friends grabbing *the N – word*,
Better than a fist in the air.
Aisha takes her power back.
After being mocked...beaten at Wingate High School, she spells
N.ow E.nlightened R.eally D.etermined.
In leather shorts. Adidas treads. Mahogany skin glowing with shea butter.
Horned-rimmed glasses. Lustrous dreads-freshly oiled.
"Queen Nerd!" She snaps, waving her three sonnets.
We raise our arms – Rocky Balboas giving a high-five;
Both of us brainy girls: parallel lines: reaching the blazing sun.

———————

The Race

It was like that time we swam outside the hotel,
Doing laps in the pool.
Tiring ourselves in the Jersey air.

How I tried so hard to beat you, flopping through
Water like fish on a stone.

But you came in first, triumphant,
And I learned to stay second.

Later, you *became* the pool,
The walls I heaved myself upon;
Your body: a bridge connecting
Two continents of life.

I held onto you, finding a new land inside your arms.
Sometimes at night, I think of the race,
Your legs zooming ahead like the ice-cream truck.
Exhaustion dangling me like a hook.

I resigned myself to following your lead.
You had looked back when you finished,
Knowing somewhere behind was the prize.

―――――

Santacon

So this is how overgrown frat boys celebrate the birth of their messiah.
Walking down the street in herds.
Some dressed as reindeer.
Wearing brown felt, animal suits
Like *plushies* waiting to get laid.
Or decked as Santas making beelines to the bars.
All over Third Avenue.
Almost all them used to be white,
But now brown and black idiots
Have joined their ranks.
And half-dressed girls,
Sashaying as elves, or
Santa's mistresses.
Some clumped like hair in a drainpipe
Clogging the sidewalk.
Keeping fellow pedestrians
From walking quickly through the
December cold.
Others drive SUVs filled with revelers
Dressed as North Pole locals.
Making spectators wonder – pray for --
A designated driver.
Misha goyem, my
Grandmother would have said:
"Crazy gentiles…look at how they worship their son of G-d!"
She would have laughed.
But she is decades gone and I am here to
Represent that scorn, that conceit.

A new herd of reindeer crosses East Twenty-fifth,
So I turn east at Twenty-fourth,
Roll my eyes.

————

Sloan Kettering

So this is what a real hospital looks like!
With friendly staff and scrubbed floors.
Carpet that's actually clean.
All the elevators work.
Uniformed workers are hired to run the panels; don't bother to press a button.

Dad's room has a window facing East 67th.
He's offered salmon, massage, and cable.

I work in a Brooklyn clinic.
Attendings are sparse as hand soap,
Priceless as the hoarded paper towels,
Hidden behind doors with Xerox paper.
The patients wait their turn for allotted treatment.

Today, Dad has stage four, and Mom discusses his sick lungs in the lounge.
I sip and tasty cup of coffee. Given scot free.
Along with the warm hug of a social worker,
Amid the comfort of polished wood furniture.

In the dense hush of insurance money,
This is closest to Heaven.

_____

Soliloquy Of The Ashkenazi

Lament of the Off-White Outcast

Mom claims we're mood rings
On the mighty fingers of Europe.
Countries changing our color
According their temperament.

Dad says we're a Rorschach test
For the gentiles.

My sister says, "No, a Rubix Cube:
Segments moving on a continent's fickle whims."

I say, "We are society's chameleon
Seeking safety."

_____

Something Larger Than Oneself

The Brotherhood Synagogue. Next to a holocaust memorial.
A long, narrow path covered in gravel, panels walling off one side.
Names etched of congregants who recently passed, joining the horribly murdered.
'Wolf' and 'Rokeach'. 'King' which my mother confides had been 'Katz' or 'Cohen'.
We look at the wall, percolating Judaism which gave a strong, robust brew.
My deceased father's name etched on a brass leaf on a Tree of Life in Jersey.
Neither Mom nor I state this. No mention needed.
Just this honor, the emblem of ancient kinship, the joy of belonging,
Quietly filled our hearts like blood, like oxygen.

———

Spinal Surgery

The pain is an expected visitor.
I tip-toe around it.
No bending, no lifting.

Friends come and clean my apartment.
I sit in a humongous chair that's fed pillows.
I dream of floating on my back on the sea.
The Mediterranean splendidly warm, a sloshing
heated bathtub, Tel Aviv's coast a smudge
to the myopic gaze.
But the pain remains certain like a
mother-in-law, an accepted fact.
Four days after surgery.
Mom says,
Healing is like walking backwards from a fire,
or taking a train from a graveyard,
Rate x Time = Distance from the origin of suffering.

———

Staff Of Life

All these years, I had chosen cupcakes, he says.
"Or eclairs. Maybe a cannoli every once in a while, if
The cream looked fresh.
I had a hankering for tarts for months", he added,
With his fingers showing how large the strawberries were,
The fruit glazed with icing.

"But then I met you.
I decided to try a roll, instead
You see, that's what you are: hardy, substantial,
And go well with everything.
Whether with a soup, or as a sandwich.
You are useful, and cost little;
Heck, you are practical to have around.
Not like those other girls: so much
Fun, but only in small measure.
That's why I stuck by you."

_____

Subway

Sometimes I want to grab a man,
Pull down his trousers on the train,
Whip out the part I need from his boxers.
Blink out fellow commuters like I'm Samantha the Witch, or a professor from Hogwarts Academy,
Because it is more ruthless dating online.
Last guy was a libertine posing as turtledove; we slept together until I Said, "I love you."
The generations play a practical joke: you're married with kids or a Spinster waiting for a hookup.
Birth control wields its double-edged sword;
Women the magic act, sliced in two;
Poetry sews back pieces.
Some call that productive.
The world outside spirals: a harlot letting down hair.
Even Penelope got back her man;
How long do the rest of us wait?

―――――

Sylvia

She was the woman who liked fine art. Loved abstracts.
Folded together her own book; red envelopes attached as pages.
See this woman on a ventilator.
And these are her daughters and the son, yes: the man never spoke
Of. He enters the ICU, commanding space, touching that female body
Not hugged in years.
See clear, plastic tubes as mandibles, cheekbone armature, grey tufts on
Her scalp uneven from when she cut off her curls -
A tossed rock sunken deep in the pillow.
Once loved Fluffy, smacked him, called EMS. Cut herself in remorse.
This is the artist without a cat, attending a program.
Every morning, nine o'clock, asked how was her night?
Last talk was long. We spoke of her mother long dead after years of
Drinking. A habit that ran in the family. Then, she revealed that she herself
Passed a liquor store last night and didn't go in.
That victory tow days before she swallowed every pill stockpiled
In her apartment.
This is me crying next to the machines, holding her swollen hand.
Telling her she is loved. The brain-dead, she is loved.

Tattoo

One weekend after the divorce
and *Cosmo* filled her house, Meg decided,
what the hell?
Sped to the tattoo parlor
faster than an ambulance.
Now she looks at the pink petals,
the apple-red center; this floral regret
climbing her left foot like a hungry ghost
from the River Styx. Slithering its serpentine
stem over nub of bone.
She can no longer get buried next to her Jewish mother. Cut off from her roots.
Tattoos banned by the Torah.
It seemed so easy to decorate skin: to draw a pretty world on empty space like
pulling a thistle crayon out of the crammed, yellow
cardboard box.
But anguish is sometimes larger than the body's surface.

The Tin Man (Arthritis)

Like flowers drop petals,
Or trees lose leaves,
the spine shrinks in cartilage,
and soon you're a Tin Man,
A stalled machine,
An inconvenience for pedestrians.
An arrow of pain shoots through,
And you're stranded on the sidewalk
Fifty feet from home.

Once so proud to live alone:
Carry your groceries,
Fix lunch,
Feed two pets,
Stoop low to clean the litterbox,
Now you're unable to take out trash:
A smell bothering the neighbors,
You are an annoyance for the super.
And now you wince when bending,
An agony lowering yourself to the toilet,
grabbing the towel rack to get back up.
Your phone number lurks on nephews'
Caller ID: No one wants to catch the message.
No one wants to hear your voice.
No kid wants to drive you around.
Who wants to take off work?
Lose vacation time or even sick days,
To take a lonely spinster to the doctor?

You paid your dues:
Taxes, the rent, utilities,
Worked forty years in the bowels of a city job
Without raising children.

Who will love you now?

———————

The Universal Church

The Spirituality Mall.
Where you could wear a bonnet,
A tiara, or bathing cap.

Have a tabby co-officiate;
Feline wandering the yard;
Bride and groom following behind.

Make up a belief system.
Design your own faith!
Just smack on your uniform like Captain Kirk,
Stroll through cyberspace.
Get ordained, free and fast!
There's no need to study, no sacrifice to make;
Become a priest in your pajamas.

Marry your next couple in a gas station bathroom.
Under a cocktail table. In a meat locker. On your living room couch.
In this church of cut-and-paste
Be your own god.

———

The Widows

They sit by the pool's edge.
Breathe in the chlorinated steam.
Legs splayed in planked, vinyl chairs.
The imprint of molded bars tattoo cellulite.
One lady wades in the heated water,
Teal walls surrounding her full, Polish hips.
These are widows that buoy up my mother.
Their gossip carrying her over the pain of
Sleeping alone in a queen-sized bed.
These are women that call the lifeguard a "slut"
Behind the girl's back.
These are the *yentas* who glance at this worker's
Heart-shaped glasses and whisper "Lolita"
Mom argues, "Lolita was a victim."
Never mind...
These non-swimmers love my surviving parent anyway.
Everyone brings novels to the pool
But who read in a crowd?

–

Yentas is a Yiddish term for women that gossip all the time.

_____

Women's March, Manhattan

These pink, two corners on
Each knitted cap.
These 'ears of a pussy'
On the heads of women and a few men.
The signs saying, "EVEN THE INTROVERTS ARE HERE."
Posters covered with illustrations of
A woman in a stars-and-stripes hijab.
The children gathered. Their parents wheel
Them in strollers, or prop them on
Wide shoulders to gather memory.
The elders walk as symbols of sacrifice:
Marching the miles in sneakers and sweat socks.
Their banners saying, "DONALD, YOU IGNORANT SLUT."
And "TRUMP HAS A TINY TOWER."
Doctors in lab coats, waving, "CARE NOT CUTS."
And, "PROTECT MEDICAID."
And me, strolling next to a woman half-Korean/half-black,
Whose parents had taken her to see Martin Luther King.
Her telling me that she first thought whites and colored
Referred to laundry, not to patrons in a restaurant.
My coaxing a restless teenage girl to relax when the
Crowd stops; that marches often stop for red lights;
That sometimes, "You stay rooted as a tree."

And then the end: the last block,
When everyone feels successful as
Completing a report or a midterm;
When responsibilities are done
And each of us can rest on our laurels,
Until the next time we are called for action.

—

*A *seder* is a long, ceremonial dinner on Passover.

Worn

I can tell you this:
I am never going back to jail, never again dating a limbless man, never losing
Another apartment to the bank.
I'm just going to be quiet. And watch *Entertainment Tonight*.

I will focus on Beyonce:
The moves. The pout. The woman who eat foie gras even it's from a dozen
Killed geese.
I picture her at home with Jay-Z and the kids, watching their ten-foot Sony.

I'm going to be just like her, and forget about dead elephants.
Murdered seals.
Drowned sharks.
Fins in some Japanese ambassador's soup.
I need Beyonce to inject me with her radiant stem cells,
Gleaned from her flashy, glitzy, vigorous brain. Pricked into my flickering,
Worn-out one. A burst of energy *a la Frankenstein, a la jumper cables*, a chance
At rebirth.
As I am so tired, so totally done.

You Ask If You Are Pretty...

I had a wife who was a knockout.
But our life was gutted my greed.
I sat in her Lexus and cried for my past,
Snagged by a radiant that disappeared,
My earnings at Lehman completely gone,
Including three thousand bucks she gave to our oldest son
For a flat screen TV and a sofa.

Twenty years back, I had shaped the helix of her life.
When I met her, she was eighteen.

Morocco was so beautiful then,
Marrakesh filled with blue light.
She cooked tripe of sheep, spiced with cumin.
Within two weeks, I spoke to her father.

Now she has the house in Teaneck.
I found a room in Newark,
And smoke out the window.
Schoolkids run track and I watch their progress.
I gain weight and vacuum the carpet.

Sometimes, you ask if you are pretty.
You stare past the table, expectant with hope.
It's been eight months of dating
And you think that means love.
I huddle against my coffee.

In 1990, my youngest slept on my chest.
He was still in diapers, five days weaned,
I secured him in the ridge of beauty,
That last joy to come from my wife;
A love you'll never know.

―――――

APPENDIX

ALPHABETICAL INDEX OF FIRST LINES

•

ROGUE SCHOLARS
Press

For General Information, go to:

http://www.roguescholars.com

For more information or a price quote for our
book design and editing services, contact:

editor@roguescholars.com

•

ROGUE SCHOLARS PRESS BOOK LIST

Awakened
Madeline Artenberg / Iris N. Schwartz
978-0-9771550-1-9

The Breakup Of My First Marriage
Bruce Weber
978-0-9771550-9-5

Expectations
Gary Beck
978-0-9840982-0-0

For Better Or Verse
Tom Guarnera
978-0-9771550-4-0

Get Over It!
Miriam Stanley
978-0-9771550-6-4

Lazarus
Jean Lehrman
978-0-9771550-5-7

Let's Fly To Trazodone
Miriam Stanley
978-0-9840982-6-2

Not To Be Believed
Miriam Stanley
978-0-9771550-3-3

Out Of And Into The Fray
Eugene Ring
978-0-9840982-1-7

Continued Other Side

A Poem Of Common Prayer
Larry Jones
978-0-9840982-2-4

————————

Anthologies:

O.O (Zero Point Zero)
Out of Print

In The Company Of Rogues
Out Of Print

Cat Breath
A Two-Headed Kitty Anthology
978-0-9771550-2-6

Estrellas En El Fuego (Stars In The Fire) - 2014
An ANYDSWPE Anthology
978-0-9840982-9-3

Shadow Of The Geode (Sombra Del Geode) - 2015
An ANYDSWPE Anthology
978-1-942463-00-9 [Bonsai Publishers, 1st Edition]

Palabras Luminosas (Luminous Words) - 2016
An ANYDSWPE Anthology
978-0-9840982-3-1

Forever Night (Siempre Noche) - 2017
An ANYDSWPE Anthology
978-0-9840982-4-8

Pa'lante A La Luz (Charge Into The Light) - 2018
An ANYDSWPE Anthology
978-0-9840982-5-5

www.ingramcontent.com/pod-product-compliance
Lightning Source LLC
LaVergne TN
LVHW041159080426
835511LV00006B/666